Self-Esteem

The Indispensable Compendium Brimming With Clandestine Knowledge On Enhancing One's Self-Assurance In Many Everyday Circumstances

(How To Overcome Poor Self-Esteem: Techniques For Increasing Self-Confidence That Have Been Scientifically Demonstrated)

Zachery Hensley

TABLE OF CONTENT

Easy But Effective Habits Of Exceptionally Happy People 1

How To Put Self-Acceptance Into Practice 28

Embracing Failure 36

Mental Visualisation Is Beneficial. 72

Overcoming Difficulties And Obstacles 78

What Is The Process Of Mind Reading? 104

Maintaining And Developing Self-Esteem 160

Examining Social Situations: Effective Communication For Self-Observers 178

Easy But Effective Habits Of Exceptionally Happy People

The happiest people aren't the richest, sharpest, or most materially fortunate ones. They have chosen to be happy, which is why they are content. A multimillionaire might be sleeping through the night in agony, while a person who doesn't even know when they will eat might be living a contented life. Being wealthy isn't the key to happiness; instead, it comes from accepting who you are and adopting a fresh perspective. We'll go over 15 straightforward but effective habits that contented individuals share below:

#1: They have no resentment

Grudges are seldom cultivated by happy individuals. They forget and forgive easily, and they don't let bad feelings cloud their positive thinking. They spare their mind and spirit from negative effects such as stress, anxiety, and sadness by not harboring grudges. They radiate positivity and have a clear conscience.

2: They show kindness to all.

According to researchers, being kind makes you happy. People who are happy stay helpful and kind. They enjoy inner peace and contentment because they treat others with love, respect, and decency.

#3: They are bold aspirants.

Contented individuals are adept at turning hardships into opportunities. They are not weighed down by issues. They hunt for answers and avoid problems because of their upbeat and optimistic mindset. Aspirations and dreams go hand in hand. Contented individuals cultivate a dream or dreams that help them stay engaged and occupied.

#4: They are unconcerned

People that are happy don't worry about little things. They believe that life is too brief to be wasted or to harbor resentment since it is so sweet. They are able to maintain their happiness since they are not burdened by anything.

#5: They respect other people

Those who are happy tend to compliment and praise other people. They also feel fantastic about themselves as a result of this. They don't pass judgment on other people or engage in gossip.

#6: They arrive on time

Researchers in psychology have found that those who are content get up early and perform other daily tasks on time. This increases their productivity and preserves their circadian rhythm, ensuring that they are content at all times.

#7: They don't make social comparisons

Happy people don't judge others based on their social standing. They treat everyone equally, which emanates optimism. They are simply different to them. By concentrating on their own development without hostility, they are content.

#8: They pick their friends carefully

People who are easygoing tend to keep their social circle small. They continue to be surrounded by enthusiastic individuals who share their views. This strengthens and sustains their inner peace. They take care to avoid having pessimistic companions that could undermine them with their pessimism.

#9: They don't try to win over people.

People who are content don't needlessly appease others. They have enough self-assurance to allow their personalities to speak for them. They don't rely on other people's superficial opinions; instead, they think for themselves.

#10: They pay close attention when they speak.

People who are happy don't talk or listen excessively, so they stay happy. They are open to the opinions of others and absorb a great deal of knowledge for their own improvement.

11: They think relationships are important.

One cannot be happy if they are lonely. People who are pleased cherish their relationships. They recognize the value of social connections and invest sufficient effort to create them, resulting in a vibrant social network.

12: They ponder and pray

Regular prayer and meditation are practices of happy individuals who cultivate inner peace. They are aware of when and how to calm their nerves by blocking out outside distractions.

13: They work out and consume wholesome meals.

Happy people eat well and exercise frequently, so they don't worry about their physical health. Their optimal energy level is determined by their mental and physical well-being.

#14: They are independent

Frivolous items do not clog the lives of happy people. They support "simple living and high thinking" and simplicity.

#15: They tell it like it is

Lying lowers one's sense of value and causes stress. Because they have a high sense of self-worth, happy people are always truthful. They don't regret being so audacious.

Permits an Alternative View of a Problem

When you're depressed, it can be difficult to stand back and consider the subject from a new angle. Engaging in conversation with others can prompt them to share their thoughts and valuable recommendations that you may not have considered.

Maybe people don't really know who to go to about their difficulties, which is one of the reasons they don't talk to anyone about them. You could wish to talk to a family member, a friend, an adult who is a little older, or perhaps a therapist. Making sense of things will be aided by talking about your feelings. It will help you sort through your emotions and clarify the problem, even if you merely chat with someone you can trust about what's upsetting you.

If you don't share information, you may have come across a scenario that appears more intricate than it actually is. Talking to someone could enable you to view the situation in a fresh or different light. There would be a slight personal impact on someone who is not involved in the event, allowing them to be more objective about what is happening. The individual you're speaking with may even offer ideas for solutions you hadn't previously considered.

The act of speaking enables us to "hear" and perceive ourselves. This gives us the power to alter our emotions and ideas. Once we hear ourselves say, "I can't handle this for one more day," we can follow up with, "If I don't get help," or "I'm going to."

Permits Assistance to Be Given to You

Therefore, isolating oneself won't be beneficial. Healthy partnerships give the support and incentive needed to conquer new and unique obstacles, even if they just listen to a supportive voice. Furthermore, you have the right to speak up when you find someone who listens to you without passing judgment when you're feeling low or angry.

Speaking also demonstrates to us that thinking and feeling are usually less dangerous when expressed aloud to others than when kept to ourselves.

Speaking with someone about your issues can also be a great way to let off steam and release tension. It will help you to put the question out of your head only. "It doesn't only feel fantastic, but it can also provide you with fresh insights on what's going on in your life." Reach out to someone who will listen when you need to talk. Still, no listener would do that anyhow. This is especially true if your stress is unpredictably high, persistent, and unsolvable—for example if you're dealing with an emotional loss from a miscarriage, a work-related difficulty, a relationship crisis, or a medical condition like being told you are infertile.

1.3 Justifications for Not Speaking

Being unable to do this comes at a much higher price than simply feeling a little uncomfortable or ashamed.

These are the top three reasons that social skills are so important in life.

Low Social Skills Come With Unexpected Costs

Although you might believe that social skills are only important for dating and parties, they are also quite important in the workplace. For some, they might be the difference between a fat paycheckand nothing at all. Financial measurements are used in the corporate world to calculate most things. The company's revenue has increased; we've been operating effectively this year. It was a poor year for the company—our staff expenses increased while our income decreased.

Unfortunately, calculating anything in monetary terms is also deceptive. Having more money than the average does not guarantee that the internal workings of the company are secure.

Consider this one instance. One of your pals has a successful tech business and was thinking about starting a tiny, one-person business. After a night of drinking, he told you what you thought of the man running the one-man operation. As a buddy, you told him straight out that you wouldn't want the guy on your team since he was much too arrogant for his expertise. Your pal canceled the order the following day. That individual will never know that his lack of social skills cost him a seven-figure salary.

It may not be a $1 million payday that you are missing, but in your office, the same thing occurs every day. At the point of evaluation, your manager looks at his boss, and they all agree that certain people are just not cut out for management. They can't even take on the most difficult assignments. If you are unable to treat people with respect, opportunities will begin to slip away from you. Shall they simply pass you by?

Leaders' Neglect Has Its Own Unexpected Costs

When a leader interacts poorly with others in the organization, a number of effects occur that are rarely evaluated. These have an impact on the manager and the company, but they are not taken into account as a direct route to the activity, and it will be very challenging to track the related costs.

But the purpose of this post is not to force you to make intricate financial projections in order to determine how much your correspondence will cost.

Rather, the focus is on increasing awareness of the importance of interaction with leadership. You need to be aware of the influence you have on your organization, whether it is good or bad.

Your Team Members Disengage When You Communicate Badly

When a leader behaves poorly, his or her team may become very irritated. Information is withheld or misrepresented, requiring team members to invest time and effort in understanding what is happening. If the key ideas aren't conveyed clearly, staff members could also feel isolated and uninvolved.

In the end, all of this results in a disgruntled worker who would sooner be anywhere else than on the squad. Disengaged employees don't operate well under some CEOs. Instead of just being fed up with their jobs, they expect them to put in more effort when the problem pertains to leadership the majority of the time. Many bosses anticipate that their staff member will change their mindset without blaming their own direction for any issues.

Negative Communication Decreases Your Team's Confidence

Ineffective communication can significantly affect each team member's confidence. When faced with an unfamiliar circumstance or difficulty solving a problem, many people tend to be very judgmental of themselves.

The employees who have low self-esteem will be the most affected. They'll be doubting their abilities and ability to succeed in their role all the time. The worst part is that their lack of faith may just stem from the fact that, given their information, *nobody* could reasonably be expected to complete the job. It has no basis in reality.

A worker who constantly questions his actions can irritate you as well as his teammates. They will also take longer to make decisions and finish tasks. It is your responsibility as a leader to foster trust wherever you can within your team. Your interactions with each other are crucial to this.

Avoid the unstated consequences of poor communication with the leadership. When managing a team, you must be conscious of the impact that your interactions have. Even if it is rarely readily observable in financial terms, it still needs to be calculated!

Make sure you comprehend the significance of the information you are delivering and the manner in which you communicate it when dealing with your personnel.

3. Paying Attention

Active listening is a mindset that embodies respect, understanding, and sincere interest in others. It is not just a method. It is the secret that opens up a conversation to its full potential and enables both participants to explore the deep waters of empathy and understanding. In the context of negotiation, let's examine the subtleties, significance, and application of active listening.

How Does Active Listening Work?

Active listening is fundamentally a completely immersive mode of hearing. It entails actively participating in the conversation and deciphering the underlying intents, feelings, and unsaid signals rather than merely listening to words. Being completely present while putting one's own agenda, prejudices, and preconceptions aside in order to fully comprehend the speaker is known as active listening.

The Foundation of Attentiveness in Active Listening This entails paying close Attention to the speaker. It entails putting away distractions, quieting inner chatter, and giving the speaker your full Attention.

- Patience: Give the speaker time to finish speaking without interjecting. Refrain from offering answers, arguments, or personal experiences right away.

-Comments: Provide comments in a non-aggressive way. To ensure correct comprehension, you can do this by nodding, making affirmations like "I see" or "I understand," or repeating back what you've heard.

- Clarification: Look for clarification if something is unclear. Posing open-ended questions can motivate the speaker to go into further detail about their arguments.

- Empathy: Acknowledge and affirm the feelings expressed by the speaker. This entails understanding and recognizing their feelings rather than necessarily agreeing with them.

Advantages of Bargaining

- Establishing Trust: The foundation of fruitful negotiations is trust, which is created by proving that you are sincerely listening to and appreciating the other party's viewpoint.

- Finding Underlying Issues: While someone is speaking, you may be able to infer underlying worries or motives from their actions.

- Reducing Misunderstandings: You can reduce the likelihood of misinterpretations that can result in conflicts by making sure you have a thorough understanding of the other party's viewpoint.

Problems and Strategies for Solving Them

- Resolving Bias: Biases exist in all of us. The secret is to recognize them and deliberately put them aside while you're actively listening.

- Refraining from Premature Solutions: It's human nature to want to offer suggestions or answers right away. But it's important to hold off on acting on this inclination until the speaker has finished speaking during active listening.

- Controlling Emotional Reactions: Conversations can get heated at times.

Emotional self-regulation exercises can support keeping the composure needed for active listening.

Useful Methods for Active Listening

- The Reflective Technique: To make sure you comprehend and demonstrate your interest, restate or paraphrase what the speaker has said.

- Open-ended Questions: These are queries that don't have a straightforward "yes" or "no" response. They promote clarity and more in-depth conversation.

-Taking notes: It can be helpful to do so during formal talks. Make sure it doesn't, however, break up the flow of the discussion.

The foundation of meaningful communication is active listening. It acts as a bridge in the context of negotiations; negotiators who are skilled in active listening provide themselves a tool that transcends simple transactional exchanges and opens the door to revolutionary, win-win solutions.

How To Put Self-Acceptance Into Practice

Self-acceptance takes time to develop; it comes from loving and caring for yourself. You become more cheerful, more anchored in the here and now, and begin to accept yourself more and more as you gain self-awareness.

To start accepting and feeling at ease with who you are, there are a few things you may do. These are the main actions that you must take:

Decide on your objective: First, make accepting yourself your goal. Take out your journal and start a new page with the words "My Journey to Self-acceptance." Next, write on it, "I am trying to be kinder to myself and fully and genuinely accept myself."

After reading this sentence out loud a few times, it will start to sink in and give you the impression that you have something you want to achieve. To maintain your attention on your objective, repeat this advice each day. Furthermore, thinking positively generates concepts that attract favorable events your way.

Have self-compassion: One of the three things that encourage self-acceptance, according to University of Hertfordshire psychologist Professor Karen Pine, is treating yourself with kindness. The other two—awareness of your strengths and spending time with yourself—will be covered in a moment.

Start being kind to yourself, acknowledge that you are a fallible person, and try not to be too hard on yourself when you make a mistake. Consider your errors as teaching moments that will help you become a better person rather than dwelling on them.

Secondly, feed your mind with sweet, loving, and upbeat thoughts to continuously inspire and motivate yourself. Say, "It's okay" if you run into difficulties while working on a task. "If I work hard and trust myself, I can eventually succeed" is a more positive statement than "I can't do it, I'm a failure."

Your abilities are honed by such encouraging self-talk, and as you get better, your self-love grows. Furthermore, NEVER call yourself names that make you feel horrible about yourself, such as "failure, loser, lost cause, stupid," or anything like that.

Having supportive and upbeat individuals around you is another crucial step in practicing self-compassion. Locate the people in your life who are controlling, manipulating, or exploiting you, and gradually cut ties with them. These small adjustments will have a positive impact on your self-perception, which will raise your level of self-acceptance.

Identify your advantages: Thirdly, identify your greatest qualities and strengths so that you can feel proud of yourself; if you are unable to do so right away, do not panic.

Since everyone has some talent, it makes sense that you would possess certain traits, abilities, and capabilities. Think about your attributes, past successes, and values to emphasize your strengths. To do this assignment, seek assistance from a helpful person. There must be a few kind, upbeat people in your life who genuinely care about you and want the best for you.

Make contact with these individuals and request their assistance in comprehending your important resources. In order to remember these attributes, make a note of them. After you've determined this, look for methods to hone them so your strengths can become abilities you can employ to accomplish your objectives. Additionally, when your assets get stronger, your self-esteem will also increase, leading to a higher degree of self-acceptance.

Spend time alone yourself well: Even only ten minutes a day should be dedicated to spending quality time with oneself. Find a quiet place to relax and pay attention to your emotions.

Allow a wide range of emotions and ideas to come and go from your head without making any snap decisions. Recall that ideas do not just randomly lodge themselves in your mind; rather, you hold a particular idea and then give it further consideration, which solidifies it. Let go of disparate ideas and cease overthinking things in order to find inner peace.

For example, when an idea arises that you did not give a project report, allow it to pass and concentrate on your breathing. When a negative thought recognizes that your mind is not its "fertile ground," it will leave your mind very fast.

Being at ease with your inner thoughts and feelings comes from spending peaceful time with yourself, and this gradually increases your self-acceptance.

Embracing Failure

There is an age-old adage that advises against surrendering, urging individuals to persevere until the very end. Similarly, an individual can only achieve victory at some juncture in their existence if they exert diligent effort to attain it. Not everyone achieves their desires just by surrendering readily. They ceased their movement just when they were on the verge of achieving victory.

The path to success is arduous, and only a select few embark upon it. In order to attain your desired outcome, it is necessary to confront challenges directly. Essays exploring the concept that mistakes are crucial for achieving success. We acquire the most knowledge from our errors. Undoubtedly, life is an arduous and protracted struggle. Individuals occasionally ponder their ability to survive until the following day. This article explores the concept that failure is an essential component of achieving success, emphasizing that both failure and success are inherent aspects of human existence.

Not all men can consistently achieve greatness in life, and thus far, none of them have been able to do so. Failures often occur unexpectedly and manifest in various ways. It can manifest as financial difficulties or health issues.

Even highly accomplished individuals often experience subsequent failures. It is important to recognize that mistakes indicate flaws in the planning process. It is analogous to a student undergoing an examination and receiving unsatisfactory marks. Perhaps he failed to adequately prepare.

Making mistakes is not inherently incorrect, but failing to derive knowledge from them is. Despite experiencing multiple failures, it is worthwhile to make another attempt. There is frequent discussion on the origins of KFC. The true narrative revolves around the many failures and hardships endured by Colonel Harland Sanders. Ultimately, however, he remains motivated after experiencing over 1000 failures. At the age of 65, he ultimately attains his desired outcome, a milestone often associated with retirement for many individuals. He remained unaffected when more than a thousand individuals expressed their dislike for his food. However, he possessed unwavering confidence in his abilities and his strategy.

Self-belief and self-assurance are also conducive to achieving success. It demonstrates the potential of diligent effort, unwavering dedication, and strong ambition. Failures provide an opportunity for a renewed attempt, characterized by increased determination, vigor, and strategic preparation. Notable figures such as Abraham Lincoln and Steve Jobs are referenced in the statement regarding how mistakes serve as the basis for achieving achievement.

They established their own niche in the globe. Abraham Lincoln experienced defeat in several formidable electoral contests. His own constituents lost faith in him. He displayed unwavering perseverance in the face of defeat. However, he persisted and displayed resilience by consistently returning with determination and courageously battling his challenges. In addition, Steve Jobs was terminated from the firm.

What are the reasons for the high rate of failure among individuals striving for success?

The more quickly you can acquire knowledge from your errors, the earlier you will comprehend that loss is an inherent aspect of life. When faced with failure, there are two courses of action available:

(1) Determine the cause of the problem and attempt to rectify it. Alternatively, (2) to ascertain that it is not feasible and move on to the subsequent concept.

Errors are an inherent component of human existence.

The reason for its failure:

Individuals often underestimate their potential for success in life.

Insufficient resolve and effort over an extended period.

Lacking humility.

If individuals are unable to establish connections and develop robust relationships.

If they are easily prone to being distracted by others

Experiencing visual impairment.

Oblivion Errors Produced in previous times. It is advisable to make irreversible decisions.

They lack sufficient self-discipline and self-confidence to have faith in their own abilities.

Failure serves as the crucial catalyst for achieving achievement.

Failure is an inherent aspect of life, yet it presents us with an opportunity to begin anew, derive lessons from our errors, and enhance our proficiency in areas where we excel. Failure might be disheartening. However, Winston Churchill imparted to us that "success is the ability to persevere through failure after failure without losing one's enthusiasm."

Failure is the primary and pivotal lesson that everyone universally acquires in life.

Enabling you to reach greater levels of achievement and broaden your perspective to consider previously unexplored opportunities.

Adversity enhances your resilience and fosters humility.

Adversity molds your character and enhances your resilience.

Failure can facilitate personal growth in three distinct manners: Maintain humility at all times, regardless of the circumstances. By acknowledging your errors, you will experience a sense of relief and be capable of setting aside your ego, enabling you to concentrate on your future endeavors.

Acknowledging faults might be distressing and seemingly insurmountable, yet endeavor to commence with a glimmer of optimism and illumination.

The desire to acquire knowledge and skills. Our failures stem from our lack of knowledge in the art of learning. Acquiring new talents is the most valuable investment you can make in your personal development.

Strategies for Achieving Your Desires

In order to achieve optimal results, it is necessary to adhere to a concise set of guidelines. The outcome varies based on the individual, as each person possesses their own unique approach to achieving success.

Devote your utmost passion and dedication to endeavors that truly resonate with your desires.

Exert substantial effort to get your desired goals. Acquiring desirable outcomes is only possible via sustained and diligent effort.

Strive to exhibit virtuous behavior and maintain a modest demeanor, regardless of the challenges it may present.

It is of greater significance to prioritize self-reflection over concerning oneself with the actions of others.

Strive to ascertain the maximum extent of your capabilities.

Make an effort to assist and motivate individuals who are in need of support.

Generate novel concepts and exhibit fearlessness in experimenting with them. The world is abundant with opportunities, and the only constraint is the atmosphere above.

The benefits of hypnosis and rebirth

Hypnosis, frequently misconstrued or undervalued, presents a remarkable range of advantages that can profoundly impact our cognition, conduct, and general welfare. Hypnosis enables us to penetrate profound levels of the mind that may be challenging to access through ordinary consciousness by inducing a guided trance state.

Hypnosis has the potential to diminish tension and anxiety, enabling profound relaxation of both the body and mind, thus facilitating the development of more efficient coping mechanisms.

Hypnosis is commonly employed as a means to aid individuals in ceasing smoking, shedding weight, or eradicating other undesirable behaviors, bolstering their resolve and inclination to enact beneficial modifications in their everyday existence.

Hypnosis can be utilized by athletes, artists, and public performers to enhance concentration, boost self-assurance, and optimize performance in demanding circumstances.

Hypnosis can facilitate the examination of the underlying causes of illogical fears and seemingly unexplainable phobias, enabling individuals to address their difficulties with a more logical mindset.

Moreover, hypnosis can provide significant assistance to individuals with insomnia or sleep disorders by facilitating a state of deeper and more rejuvenating sleep.

Hypnosis can alleviate both chronic and acute pain by altering pain perception and producing a feeling of calm.

In addition, hypnosis can enhance self-esteem and self-confidence, fostering a favorable and supportive self-perception.

Hypnosis provides access to the unconscious mind, unveiling concealed ideas, feelings, and memories that might aid in self-awareness.

This method can provide significant assistance to those experiencing migraines and other pain-related conditions, effectively diminishing the frequency and severity of their symptoms.

Overall, hypnosis can enhance overall wellbeing, foster heightened self-awareness, and cultivate a more stable emotional equilibrium.

Nevertheless, these advantages are but a small fraction of the numerous benefits that hypnosis can provide. When utilized with responsibility and under the supervision of skilled practitioners, hypnosis can serve as a valuable instrument for accessing the untapped potential of the mind and enhancing different facets of everyday existence.

Simultaneously, rebirthing provides a distinctive avenue to achieve mental and emotional wellness by engaging in mindful breathing exercises. Practicing this profound technique of breathwork can facilitate the liberation of accumulated tensions, resulting in a transformative inner renewal.

The practice of rebirth breathwork facilitates the release of suppressed emotions, tensions, and accumulated stress in both the physical and mental realms, resulting in a sense of relaxation and buoyancy.

Engaging in the deliberate act of inhaling throughout the process of being born again can have a substantial impact on diminishing stress and anxiety, providing profound relaxation, and enhancing emotional equilibrium.

Moreover, rebirth presents the chance to delve into previous experiences and confront unresolved incidents or traumas, enabling a fresh outlook and a route toward emotional restoration.

Engaging in deliberate respiration during the process of rebirth can contribute to the stabilization of one's mood and enhancement of emotional equilibrium, ultimately resulting in heightened inner tranquility.

Rebirth facilitates a profound state of consciousness, enabling you to forge a more profound bond with your own being and your own realm.

Rebirthing is the act of engaging in the practice of rejuvenation. Practicing breathwork helps alleviate muscular and physical stress, enhancing general bodily comfort and facilitating relaxation.

Rebirth facilitates the cultivation of a more profound comprehension of respiration, enhancing pulmonary capacity and augmenting oxygenation within the organism.

The concept of reincarnation can facilitate individual development by encouraging introspection and consciousness, hence creating opportunities for profound change.

Reincarnation can result in enhanced self-acknowledgment and heightened compassion towards oneself and others.

In general, rebirth can enhance overall wellbeing by strengthening the link between the mind and body and fostering better inner peace.

Practicing rebirth breathing can have a substantial impact on lowering tension and anxiety, promoting profound relaxation, and enhancing emotional equilibrium.

Moreover, rebirth offers a chance to delve into previous experiences and address unresolved occurrences or traumas, enabling a fresh outlook and route toward emotional restoration.

Engaging in deliberate and mindful respiration during the process of being born again can contribute to the stabilization of one's emotional state and enhance emotional equilibrium, ultimately resulting in heightened inner tranquility.

Rebirth facilitates a profound state of consciousness, enabling you to forge a more profound bond with your own being and your own realm.

RebirthingBreathwork is a therapeutic technique that can alleviate muscular and physical tension, enhancing overall bodily comfort and facilitating relaxation.

Rebirth facilitates the cultivation of a more profound comprehension of respiration, enhancing pulmonary capacity and augmenting oxygenation within the organism.

Engaging in the practice of rebirth can facilitate individual development by encouraging introspection and mindfulness, thereby creating opportunities for profound change.

Rebirth can result in enhanced self-acceptance and heightened empathy, both towards oneself and others.

Rebirth can enhance overall wellbeing by bolstering the connection between the mind and body and fostering increased inner harmony.

Exercise Gratitude

Gratitude is a highly effective technique for boosting confidence and self-worth, and it has a profound effect on our general well-being and well-being. Acknowledging and cherishing the good things in our lives, no matter how minor is the essence of gratitude. By concentrating on the positive aspects of our lives, we can raise our self-esteem and confidence levels and cultivate a more optimistic outlook.

Several research studies have demonstrated the link between increased mental health and wellbeing and cultivating thankfulness. For instance, a study that was published in the Journal of Happiness Studies discovered that those who wrote letters of thankfulness expressed greater levels of life satisfaction and happiness than those who wrote about unfavorable situations or just ordinary occurrences.

There are innumerable examples of people in real life who have benefited by practicing thankfulness in addition to this scholarly research. For example about, a woman named Samantha, who is in her 30s, revealed how practicing thankfulness altered her life. I'm not sure where I read it. She felt as though nothing in her life was going right because she had been battling depression and anxiety for years. She did, however, observe a noticeable change in her attitude on life and mood after beginning a daily appreciation practice.

She eventually started to see the wider picture from a much more positive and empowered perspective and developed a deeper appreciation for the little pleasures in life, like her daily cup of coffee or lunch dates with friends. Later on, Samantha said she felt a lot more certain and upbeat about her life in general, as well as her future.

Exercise for boosting confidence:

Every day, find three things for which you are thankful, no matter how tiny, and write them down.

This is the reason why.

A quick and easy technique to foster thankfulness and boost confidence and self-worth is to set aside some time each day to compose a brief list of things for which you are grateful. It is possible to consciously direct our attention away from unfavorable ideas and emotions by concentrating on the positive aspects of our existence. We may feel happier and more upbeat as a result, which will ultimately strengthen our sense of contentment and self-worth.

In conclusion, cultivating thankfulness is a powerful strategy for boosting confidence and self-worth. Its effectiveness is demonstrated by several real-life examples, and research has indicated that it can result in enhanced mental health and wellbeing. One easy way to cultivate thankfulness and benefit from this incredibly potent practice is to set aside some time each day to compose a brief list of things for which you are grateful. wellbeingsitive Affirmations

We have a propensity to believe almost everything we tell ourselves, which can be both positive and harmful depending on what our inner voice is telling us. It literally has the capacity to either empower and uplift us or to stifle and imprison us. The voice inside you has the power to practically shape every part of your life. It can be your greatest ally, confidante, and motivator, or it can be your deadliest enemy.

You may practically retrain your brain to think in a more empowering and positive way by utilizing affirmations if your inner voice is critical, restrictive, negative, or skeptical. Affirmations are essentially positive phrases that assist you in setting intentions for the kind of person you want to be and the emotions you want to experience. If you find it difficult to be confident, try telling yourself an affirmation like "I am courageous and confident," either out loud or quietly. As you tell yourself the affirmation as often as you can, it will eventually get ingrained in your subconscious!

Affirmations are a potent technique that women may use to rewire their brains and improve their confidence, self-esteem, and self-image. Repeating positive affirmations to yourself with the intention of altering your ideas and beliefs is known as an affirmation. Affirmations can help reorganize the brain by replacing negative ideas and beliefs with positive ones when they are used consistently.

Affirmations have the capacity to change our thoughts and beliefs, which in turn affects our feelings, actions, and results. Affirmations have been demonstrated in studies to lower anxiety and depression, raise happy feelings, and improve self-esteem.

For instance, employing affirmations boosted the confidence and self-esteem of women in a case study who had poor self-esteem. "I am worthy" or "I am enough" were among the self-worth affirmations that the participants were instructed to repeat. After just one week of repeating these affirmations, the participants reported feeling more confident and self-assured, and their self-esteem levels climbed dramatically.

Furthermore, research has discovered that affirmations can also modify the way our brain receives information. When we repeat affirmations consistently, the brain starts to believe the positive claims, which affects the way it interprets information. This process of reprogramming the brain can help us overcome negative thought patterns, build self-belief, and eventually boost our self-esteem and confidence.

In conclusion, utilizing affirmations can be a highly useful approach to improving self-esteem, self-image, and confidence in women. Whether you're battling with poor self-esteem or negative body image or simply need a confidence boost, affirmations can help you rewire your brain, change negative thoughts to positive ones, and raise your self-worth and confidence. Try repeating affirmations every day and discover the great impact they may have on your life.

Tips for Coping with Jealousy

There are several strategies to manage jealousy. Jealousy is a natural human emotion and happens in any relationship. It happens to families, couples, and friends. It is crucial to deal with it in a sensible way because if you act inappropriately about it, it may damage you and your relationships. Follow the methods to control episodes of jealousy in this article.

•If you are with your boyfriend and he chats with another girl, you should just relax and do something else to distract yourself. This will keep you from doing or saying anything you will regret later on. You can talk to someone or look for something you can do as you wait for the conversation of your companion to end.

This will distract you and make you put any feelings of jealousy or resentment aside. •It would also be great if you spoke logically with your partner about anything that made you envious. Make sure you discuss it with them alone in your house where no one can hear you. Be calm and explain how you feel. Ask him or her to be sensitive to your feelings and to never allow such a thing to happen again.

•People who usually feel jealous have very low self-esteem. It shows they have much insecurity about themselves. If you are one such kind of guy, you must find activities that will make you feel good about yourself. You can learn a new and enjoyable hobby, do regular workouts, do some gardening, which is therapeutic, or get a makeover.

•Focus on yourself instead of your partner or the person who makes you feel jealous. Remember to love yourself always. Remind yourself also that you are a beautiful person inside and out. If you always find yourself becoming jealous of even small things, this is not healthy. Get a hold of yourself and forget all suspicions crossing your mind. You may ruin your relationship instead of fixing it. You can overlook a jealous fit by concentrating on other things such as work, an ongoing conversation around you, or the ingredients you need to cook for dinner.

- When you feel jealous, avoid alcohol, as this makes you more irritated, insecure, and confrontational. Redirect your feelings to something positive by thinking about good times or things that make you happy. You can also exercise, as working out releases endorphins or feel-good hormones, which help in coping with jealousy.
- If you think your jealousy is already destroying your relationship, you better go to a psychologist and get counseling therapy. This will help save your relationship from being wrecked. An expert therapist will be able to take you to the origin of your problem. He will also be able to address your insecurities and help you build your confidence.

Jealousy is not abnormal. Just because you feel jealous does not mean you are less of a person. The most important thing is you address issues that make you envious so that things will be normal in your relationship. As long as you are sincere in coping with jealousy, everything will be okay.

Mental Visualisation Is Beneficial.

Imagination is a powerful and thought-provoking tool that each of us possesses; it is something we may use on a daily basis. You can use your individual ideas, perceptions, ideas, and gut feelings to make beneficial adjustments in your daily life that enhance every aspect of your being. All of us can create useful pictures in our brains with a little practice, even though some of us have more vivid imaginations that come to life more rapidly than others.

utilizing one's imagination as a tool

The only person who can restrict how much you can make each day from utilizing your creativity is yourself. You can envision a great deal of things with your imagination, and you can use it in almost any situation. In order to effectively use visualization, you need to first form a positive mental image of how a scenario will end, then picture this positive ending as though it is already happening in your mind, and finally, let this positive mental image replace any negative thoughts you may have previously held. You must work on the image as much as you can, considering it from all angles. It is important to have a very clear mental image of how you want the situation to play out. Consider your imagination and the mental image you form as a foundation upon which you can expand and grow, just like an architect uses a blueprint to plan a project from the ground up.

The foundation of all things

The degree of planning and preparation you put into the basis of your idea or whatever it is that you wish to modify in your mind will directly affect your capacity to succeed. Start with a rough drawing of your idea or the thing you want to change in your head and work your way up from the bottom until you can clearly see every single detail of the concept. The following should be kept in mind when you lay the foundation:

- What particular goals or changes do I want to make in my life?

- What kind of an impact will this have?

Is it feasible for me to achieve my goals on my own?

What areas of my life do I need to work on to achieve this?

- What abilities must I develop in order to succeed in this endeavor?

After you have laid the foundation for whatever it is that you wish to change in your life, you can then build on your plan, making sure that you mentally construct an accurate picture of the project's progression from start to finish and that you visualize the project's process as clearly as possible at each stage. Once your mental visualization is complete, you may start taking action to realize your goals. You can then, if you'd like, put down on paper the steps you mentally followed to get the desired result and follow them through to the finish. After completing the mental visualization, you can start taking action to realize your goals.

The key elements

When trying to employ mental imagery effectively in any area of your life, the most crucial things to keep in mind are as follows:

● Focusing your creative energy on one notion at a time ● Forming as distinct mental image as you can for the concept and its result ● Building the concept from its foundation to its conclusion

● Executing your plan with distinctiveness

Overcoming Difficulties And Obstacles

Understanding that difficulties and setbacks are a natural part of life is crucial for developing the proper mindset. These are the assessments that gauge how resilient we are and how strong our attitude is. This will cover methods and approaches to overcome barriers and difficulties, such as coping with failures, responding to criticism and rejection, developing resilience, and transforming adversity into opportunity.

Handling Obstacles

Any trip will inevitably encounter setbacks, which can truly test our mental fortitude. Our trajectory is frequently determined by how we handle adversity, whether it be a personal or professional setback. Here's how to handle failures in an efficient manner:

1. Recognise Your Emotions: Recognising your feelings is crucial when you experience a loss. Feelings of disappointment, irritation, or even grief are normal. Give yourself permission to feel these feelings without passing judgment.

2. Preserve Perspective: Evaluate the situation in light of the setback. Consider the question, "Will this setback matter in a month, a year, or five years?" Even obstacles that appear insurmountable at

the time often lose significance with time.

3. Take Lessons from the Experience: Every misstep teaches you something important. Consider the things that went wrong and the lessons you can draw from the situation. Turn setbacks into chances for development and advancement.

4. Remain Resilient: Being resilient means being able to overcome hardship. Keep your faith in your skills and your dedication to your objectives. Remind yourself that obstacles are transitory and that you possess the inner fortitude to surmount them.

5. Seek Support: When faced with obstacles, don't be afraid to get in touch with friends, mentors, or a support system. Talking to others about your struggles can help you get new insights and emotional relief.

6. Concentrate on Solutions: Move your attention from moping over the setback to really identifying solutions. What actions may you take to proceed? Divide the issue into smaller, more doable tasks.

7. Keep a Positive Attitude: When facing obstacles, your attitude is your most valuable resource. Remain optimistic and never forget that obstacles present

chances to show your tenacity and resolve.

Managing Rejection and Criticism

In life, criticism and rejection are unavoidable, particularly when aiming for pleasure and success. Your mood and capacity to move on can be greatly impacted by how you respond to rejection and criticism. Here's how to deal with them successfully:

1. Distinguish Positive from Negative Criticism: Not all criticism is the same. Recognize the difference between unjustified negativity and constructive criticism, which provides insightful input for advancement. Pay attention to the criticism that can make you better.

2. Preserve Your Self-Confidence: If you allow criticism, it can undermine your self-assurance. Remind yourself of your triumphs and your strong points. Have faith in your skills and resist the urge to allow criticism to make you feel less valuable.

3. React, Don't React: When someone criticizes you, pause for a bit before answering. Uncontrollably reacting might intensify confrontations. Instead of only responding emotionally, consider your response and address the current situation.

4. Actively Seek Feedback: Don't wait for negative feedback to approach you. Actively seek out input from reliable

people who can offer insightful criticism. By using this method, you can find areas that need work before they become contentious issues.

5. Turn Rejection into Motivation: Getting rejected is frequently a necessary step towards success. Rejection is a motivator to prove yourself and accomplish your goals instead of lingering on it. Many successful people had to overcome rejection in order to realize their goals.

6. Take Lessons from Rejections: Rejections can teach us important things. Consider the reasons behind your rejection and what you can do better the

next time. Take rejection as a chance to better yourself.

7. Keep a Growth Mindset: Adopt a growth mindset, which is the conviction that you can improve your skills with hard work and persistence. Having a growth mentality makes it easier to see rejection and criticism as chances for improvement rather than as setbacks.

Are any of those answers recognizable to you? Given the way our brains are wired, it is not shocking if they do. We have been accustomed to recognizing warning signs in order to protect our survival ever since the times when we had to constantly be vigilant in a dangerous world.

Old habits die hard, and although we no longer require that elevated state of awareness, it's simply the brain's method of ensuring our safety. The issue is that dwelling on the unpleasant aspects of life can negatively impact your relationships, mental health, and ability to make decisions.

Although we can't completely eliminate that pessimistic tendency.

In actuality, you become the person you think you are, so if you have a bad self-perception, that is precisely who you will become. Conversely, by embracing positive self-talk, you can start to improve your perception of yourself, form stronger relationships, and find greater enjoyment in life. It isn't about making up a fanciful, false self-image. It's all about loving, respecting, and accepting who you are, and you may start by putting these tactics to use:

Change the storyline

It will take some getting used to hearing that critical voice in your brain every time you do or say something, so it's not an easy task. You will instinctively begin reviewing the events that followed and regret not saying or doing certain things. Simply stop as soon as you recognize that you are falling down that rabbit hole. Since the past is gone and cannot be changed, consider how you might respond in a similar circumstance in the future. This is an illustration of what I mean:

I wanted to showcase my cooking prowess to my pals, so I asked them over for a Mexican night. Unfortunately, no one could eat the con carne since I added entirely too much chili powder to it.

Naturally, they all gave it a heartfelt chuckle and claimed it was no big deal. This could have gone one of two ways: either I laugh about it and tell myself to go easy on the chili powder the next time, or I instantly tell myself that I am reckless, thoughtless, and an incredibly lousy cook. If I followed my initial course of self-criticism, it would confirm my preexisting notions about my recklessness and make me reconsider planning an event of this nature in the future. I'll eventually convince myself that I'm incompetent, which will negatively impact my ability to succeed in the future when I encounter challenges.

A tad excessive? I agree, yet our pessimistic mindset operates in this way. It connects the dots and ultimately determines what you do and doesn't don't do in life, influencing your relationships and sense of value. Considering that, I would rather just laugh it off and perhaps cook Italian the next time!

Tell a narrative that's optimistic.

Your description of your life and identity reveals a lot about how you have shaped that self-perception. Your inner voice can start telling you that you're to blame or that you brought it upon yourself when anything "bad" happens to you. Don't believe that the majority of life's events are beyond our control, and what matters is how we respond to them, not who is at fault. Optimistic people will learn from their mistakes and have a far healthier approach to handling bad luck or accidents. Instead of sitting around thinking about what went wrong, they concentrate on getting back on track and making things right. Give your story a happy conclusion as well because that's how you will feel, not just doom and gloom.

Put action before thought.

When we are not physically moving, our brain begins to take over. Being a brain, it finds all of this vacant space to occupy and seeks to contribute. You need to take action in the now if you find yourself dwelling on the past or worrying about the future. Instead of giving room for bad ideas to arise, take an active role and give it your whole attention. Anything from taking a stroll to visiting the neighborhood mall could be included. You will experience instant benefits if you take the necessary steps to break away from unfavorableconversations. Any type of physical activity diverts your brain's attention to other tasks, allowing you to unwind and find some tranquility from your inner critic.

Savour the here and now.

Though you may be sick of hearing about mindfulness's many benefits, there's a good reason for its success. Recall that I mentioned that unpleasant memories tend to stick with us longer than happy ones. Resetting that balance can help your brain become accustomed to more positive experiences, which will ultimately balance out the negative ones. Although you cannot alter the past, you can influence the present, which is a fantastic chance to surround yourself with good energy.

The unpleasant memories will gradually fall from your long-term memory's hierarchy as you start to fill them with happy ones. We are aware that if you savor an experience in the present and play it back to yourself multiple times, it will become ingrained in your long-term memory. This is a great tool to have on hand for times when you are feeling down about yourself.

The anterior cingulate cortex is a highly judgemental region of your brain that is devoted to negative thought. This section is in charge of your feelings and is designed to react to other people's needs in an efficient manner. According to some research, women's brains have a slightly larger area dedicated to this function than do men's, which means that women are naturally endowed with an extra superpower: greater emotional sensitivity.

Depending on your perspective, either a blessing or a curse may result from this. I don't want to suggest that gender and biology play a major role here because, in general, the differences between a man's and a woman's brain are minuscule. Let's just sum up by saying that if women react more emotionally than males do, this could be a biological trait as well as influenced by a number of other things like our upbringing, character, and, of course, social conditioning.

I do know for sure, though, that having your inner critic telling you all the time how stupid, ugly, fundamentally defective, and unlovable you are may lead to a lot of worry and negatively impact your stress levels. It's understandable that you might experience stress, depression, or emotional depression if that voice in your head is constantly criticizing you for what you think are your shortcomings, downplaying your accomplishments, and instilling self-loathing.

The illusion your mind has built about your abilities and potential is what sustains every bad self-perception you have ever experienced.

That is not your fault, and I do not mean to be critical. All you have to do is start loving yourself and practice self-talk that is kind, caring, supportive, and compassionate. You should speak to yourself in the same manner that you do with your loved ones. Do you criticize them for their errors, offer depressing comments, bring up their previous transgressions, and purposefully induce feelings of guilt, humiliation, or rage in them? You will undoubtedly say "NO," so why are you harming yourself in that way? Consider it.

You can now get started! The time has arrived to take on your task, no matter how big or small, with your diary ready and your carefully selected support system in place. Among them are goals like "losing 10 pounds in three months," "waking up at six a.m. every day to run for 20 minutes," "writing 10,000 words a month for my book," and "learning Spanish to the point where I can hold a basic conversation with a native speaker on a basic topic within 12 months." Do you see how these objectives are quantifiable, targeted, and specific?

Begin Small

Divide your aim into manageable portions to maximize your performance and prevent using up your willpower too soon. Our motivation comes from little victories! If you set your sights on something exceedingly large, you probably won't get there very quickly or make much progress in that direction. Smaller things make you feel more positive and upbeat since you can cross them off as completed. This is especially helpful if, at the start of your journey, your objective feels overwhelming or even unachievable.

It's similar to eating an elephant—you have to eat it one piece at a time and aren't permitted to peek at how much is left!

For instance, during the first week of your workout regimen, start with a 5-minute run before work every weekday. From there, increase to a 10-minute run every day, then a 20-minute run every other day, etc. Alternatively, swap out your daily chip snacks for nuts for a week; master the Spanish verb "to be" and complete all the grammar book assignments related to it.

This strategy's appeal is that you can count on experiencing some success to celebrate. Furthermore, as you advance, you won't maintain a permanent state of diminished willpower. You'll feel tremendous pride and satisfaction in yourself as you accomplish each mini-goal, which will position you well for the next move.

Experience Nuclear Days

Set aside a special day every now and then to devote a brief, laser-like focus to your project in order to truly "nuke" it! Here, "short" is a crucial term. No longer than a day (or perhaps a few hours; at that point, cease). It's crucial to avoid overexerting yourself because this can lead to fatigue and, eventually, demotivation.

Your objectives for "Nuking" could include writing down every crazy idea you have for your book during a three-hour brainstorming session in your room, spending the entire afternoon immersed in Spanish with your Spanish-speaking friend and his family, or dedicating the entire morning to practicing your favorite song on the guitar. The purpose of this is to reward yourself for completing a task, inspire creative outbursts, and increase your motivation by observing your progress afterward. Recall: resume your regular schedule after it's ended.

Give yourself a reward!

The lengthy lag between the work you're doing at any given moment and the moment when the final reward of an accomplished objective arrives can easily demotivate us when we have goals, especially those that will be accomplished at some point in the future. Therefore, take a shortcut to keep yourself motivated by rewarding yourself at specific stages of the route simply for taking the necessary steps. For instance, it can take months before you feel the full benefits of starting an exercise regimen. Thus, as you perspire profusely, consider this: "I'm running because I'm excited about the reward I have planned for myself at the end of my 30 minutes." It could be something tangible, like a new pair of sneakers, or something basic, like a favorite dish or movie. After all, it could take a while until you find exercise enjoyable on its own.

Happiness is one factor that can help us strengthen our willpower. You have to be enjoying yourself while working! In order to be certain that you are acting for the right reasons, you should have already identified what it is that truly drives you and documented it in your mission statement. Now that you've got going remember to congratulate yourself when you shed your first five pounds or avoid being overdrawn within a month. Now exercise caution—I'm not saying go crazy and ruin all of your hard work! Instead, tell a reliable friend, spend the entire Sunday watching your favorite show, or go on a little trip. Choose a happy activity that aligns with your objective.

What Is The Process Of Mind Reading?

What subconscious tactics do we employ to infer the thoughts or emotions of others? There are numerous methods, although two of them are predominant. In general, we either draw from our previous encounters with them or presume that they possess similar thought processes as us. Let us examine both of these potentialities.

Experiential Terrain

You make predictions about the behavior of certain individuals in current situations based on your interpretations of your past interactions with them. If you encounter an individual who appears to be temperamental upon initial meeting, you may utilize this assessment to anticipate her future conduct as well. Perhaps during your initial encounter, she was experiencing a challenging period and is often not prone to mood swings.

Mind reading occurs by selecting a file from your collection of experiences with a person and interpreting that file during storage and retrieval.

One may make assumptions, such as assuming that the current scenario is exactly the same as the previous one or that the individual has remained unchanged over time. This is a method by which we are able to discern the thoughts of individuals.

Thought Projection

Another method of mind reading involves the act of projecting our own ideas and emotions onto other individuals. Assuming I do not derive pleasure from observing a cricket match and you happen to be a cricket enthusiast, Upon entering the living room, I noticed you engrossed in a match and expressed my sympathy, remarking, "I apologize for the lack of entertainment value in this particular telecast." You will undoubtedly be taken aback as I have entirely overlooked the fact that you derive pleasure from observing the sport of cricket. It is not mandatory to watch. Now, here's an interesting question: Who would have viewed a cricket match if no other programs were being broadcast? Indeed, I am the one you are referring to.

Our thoughts serve as the foundation for our perception of another person's thoughts in a specific situation. It is possible that you have also seen this in your own life. If someone forms an opinion on your behalf that is completely inaccurate, you have two options: either correct the individual or choose to remain silent, as explaining the truth may seem unimportant. Regardless, you experience a sense of being misunderstood.

This is the process via which misunderstandings unfold. It is possible to assume that by expressing specific words or actions, the individual under consideration will experience a sense of being valued. Regrettably, our attempt to make a gesture of goodwill has had an unintended negative consequence, causing the individual to feel unappreciated, which has left us feeling perplexed. We have attributed our preferences and aversions to him, presuming that he has our characteristics, although this may not necessarily be true.

The notion of telepathy allows us to recognize that we are not always privy to the thoughts someone else may have regarding us. Our apprehensions may simply be a product of our own interpretation of how others perceive us.

What is the purpose of mind reading?

The Unease We Feel Towards Inconclusive Narratives

Have you ever experienced a situation where you misplaced an item and found yourself unable to cease searching for it despite being pressed for time to attend another engagement on your agenda? Did you repeatedly check your phone while being occupied, eagerly anticipating a response to a message? The unknown captures our attention, particularly when there is something significant at risk. In order to prevent our energy from being depleted, it is imperative that we finalize our narratives, even if only within our own thoughts, as otherwise, they persist in a repetitive cycle.

Consider the multitude of unfinished cycles that you harbor within yourself, considering the fact that you engage with numerous individuals in your daily existence. What was the reason for your teammate's failure to respond to your phone call? What caused your friend to undergo a transformation over time? What was the reason for your exclusion from a significant decision-making process? It is unattainable to ascertain the thoughts of every individual in any given circumstance.

When the stakes are elevated, the preoccupation with seeking the perspectives of others intensifies. We can go the extra distance to attain clarity by consulting those who are involved and may possess superior knowledge, using probing inquiries to facilitate understanding, or attentively observing the unfolding events. Any action that alleviates our state of uncertainty would be beneficial.

The human mind grapples with the task of assigning significance to objects and experiences, as the absence of these clues would leave us uncertain about how to navigate our existence in this world. If I am uncertain about someone's affinity for my presence, I will be unable to determine whether it is appropriate for me to initiate a phone contact with them. Without knowledge of my boss's preferences, I will be unable to determine the appropriate course of action to secure a promotion.

While it may not be feasible for me to approach every individual and enquire, "I harbor uncertainties regarding your level of interest in spending time with me," the inherent need for understanding persists. What is the next course of action? Our highly adept mind, skilled in the art of imaginative composition, swiftly intervenes and reassures us, proclaiming, "Fear not, for I am fully capable of handling this situation!" I surmise that this individual harbors a dislike towards you, as seen by their lack of a grin at your last encounter. Regularly sending emails to your supervisor demonstrates your diligent work ethic, which is appreciated by him. That is the most probable explanation for why he would grant someone a promotion. Although without empirical data, you have discovered a method to comprehend the occurrences in your surroundings. These interpretations are telepathic in nature and may be a result of the projection of your own thoughts.

Mastering the ability to control one's projections is a highly valuable skill, particularly for individuals employed as coaches or counselors. As a coach, it is crucial for me to recognize the extent to which my interpretations are influenced by the client's perspective against my own personal ideas and biases. This is important because each client is distinct and separate from me.

Understanding What Determines Self-Esteem

Self-esteem refers to our personal evaluation of ourselves and our convictions, which in turn shape our actions. This viewpoint on self-esteem is based on cognitive behavioral therapy (CBT), which emphasizes that our interpretation of our triggers influences our thoughts and subsequent reactions to our surroundings. Possible triggers can encompass various factors such as circumstances, experiences, relationships, individuals, locations, and occurrences.

Hence, Cognitive Behavioural Therapy (CBT) instructs us that our beliefs and emotions regarding ourselves directly influence our actions and behaviors. It is essential to consider this process when analyzing the development of our self-esteem, including the factors that contribute to its health or unhealthiness.

During our early stages of life, we tend to prioritize our physical characteristics and social status when perceiving ourselves. For instance, I am an attractive young woman; I am a sibling who is older than others, or I am the youngest offspring in my family.

However, as time progresses, our perspective on life expands, and we engage in more interactions with others. As we age, our range of experiences broadens, as does the variety of people we interact with.

Each of these events and connections possesses the capacity to shape our beliefs and emotions regarding our own selves. What is the reason behind our instinctive inclination to adhere to this pattern?

By experiencing various life events and forming connections with others, we gain insight into our own attributes, inclinations, capabilities, talents, preferences, interests, and lack of interest, as well as how others perceive these same qualities and behaviors. We also acquire knowledge about the specific character traits, personal attributes, and skills that are regarded as significant by individuals in our social circle and the broader community.

Subsequently, we respond to these encounters with thoughts, feelings, and patterns of behavior. For instance, we initiate the formation of thoughts and perceptions regarding our individual identity.

- Whether we have a positive attitude towards, fully accept, and provide assistance to our own individuality.

- The question of our self-perceived worth.

Our self-perception will be influenced by the nature of these ideas, leading to either positive or negative feelings about ourselves.

Arrogance, timidity, and obsessiveness are personality traits that can potentially heighten the likelihood of developing low self-esteem. Nevertheless, it is important to acknowledge that possessing a specific personality trait that may contribute to diminished self-esteem does not automatically imply the development of low self-esteem.

Thus far, you have acquired knowledge regarding diverse factors that mold our cognition and emotions towards our own selves, and you have discerned which of these factors are applicable to you. Keep in mind that although these things may have negatively affected you and your self-esteem in the past, they do not necessarily have to continue to do so in the future.

What is the impact of your past on your self-esteem?

Each encounter in life possesses the capacity to influence our cognitive perception and, subsequently, our self-esteem. However, specific encounters are more prone to adversely affect our self-esteem as they may prompt us to doubt ourselves and our abilities, feel uncertain, or perceive these experiences as implying something unfavorable about us.

Adversities encompass various distressing or burdensome encounters, such as harassment.

• Dissolution of parental union.

• Presence of violence and abuse within your surroundings.

• Personal or collective calamities.

• Medical conditions and potential harm to oneself or others.

- Terminating romantic relationships.

When striving for a strong sense of self-worth, it can be beneficial and essential to reflect on your past experiences in order to gain a deeper understanding of your present behaviors, habits, and idiosyncrasies. The visual and auditory stimuli that children are exposed to significantly influence their development and behavior. Individuals who are raised by parents who provide support and compassion or those who observe acts of generosity, tolerance, and kindness tend to possess heightened sensitivity towards the emotional conditions and welfare of others.

The development of your personality and self-esteem during adolescence is shaped not only by the knowledge imparted by your parents, guardians, and relatives but also by the observations and experiences derived from their behaviors. The influence of your family is paramount in shaping your self-esteem and influencing your personal growth over the course of your life.

Individuals raised in an unsupportive household or with neglectful carers are prone to developing diminished self-worth in their future years. You may have a tendency to depend on the validation of others, whether through spoken or unspoken means, in order to determine your behavior. It is likely that you are engaging in this behavior without conscious awareness, and you may not realize that you are being influenced by something that originated in your early childhood.

Recall the exceptional educators who have nurtured, aided, stimulated, and directed you toward a sound comprehension of the world. Whenever you feel confident about accomplishing something positive, their names readily spring to mind. It would be ideal if all guardians could exhibit such behavior. You likely recall individuals who ridiculed, insulted, and instilled in you a sense of unworthiness whenever you encountered fear or trauma. These external factors are impeding your progress towards developing a healthier sense of self-worth. They were shaping numerous aspects of your self-perception, whether you were aware of it at the time or not.

This straightforward example clearly demonstrates the direct correlation between your past experiences and their impact on your self-esteem. It is imperative to grant forgiveness to both others and oneself and release any lingering attachments.

Mental tranquility.

Being happy and using that as a primary indicator of your mental health is the true test of success. When you equate material possessions, concepts, and beliefs with happiness. Sometimes, though, real happiness comes from within, and you have to let go of everything that can disturb your sense of inner peace and contentment because you are so consumed with things that only serve to benefit the outside world.

Some of these external and external factors drive you crazy, such as how they impact your physical and mental well-being. Keeping you up at night, too. You have to let them go because they have been there for too long—it's like driving for four hours—and they are hot. The engine will be hot, of course.

Therefore, you need to stop and allow it to settle by overcoming negative feelings, of which blame is the main destroyer. You have to learn to move past it and move on.

Everybody has, at some point in their lives, dealt with hurtful criticism, unfavorablebehavior, rudeness, unfairness, betrayal, and dishonesty from others. Although these are regrettable, they are an inevitable aspect of being a human.

However, a straightforward question to ask after a bad experience is, "How long will it take me to get over this event and get on with my life?" If you want to be truly happy in life, this is one of the most important decisions you will ever have to make. This is a decision that only you can make. It is an assessment of your capacity for mental, spiritual, and forgiving forgiveness.

In therapy, every psychologist and psychiatrist who works with unhappy patients always discuss what someone did or didn't do for them or to them in the past and how unhappy the patient is still about it.

You have to realize how brilliant your mind is. Your mind can be used to your advantage to help you be joyful and content, or it can be used against you.

Use your intelligence to assign blame and let go of the unpleasant circumstance rather than replay and analyze a past incident in an attempt to find excuses and reasons to take it personally because one of your most valuable possessions—beyond your imagination—is your peace of mind.

Instead of arguing and stating what he wasn't and who he was, Steve Harvey was mistaken for a musician by someone who didn't even give him a chance to explain himself. Steve simply acknowledged that he was the musician the man was referring to. Steve had just rescued himself from an altercation, hurt feelings, and rudeness. He just took it as it was.

Making and forming relationships with people who accept you for who you are and who you feel comfortable with in your own skin is another necessary component of happiness. Being in the company of individuals who respect and value you brings you more than just mental calm. You feel good about yourself and content when you're around them. For instance, you become more efficient and appear to be more productive than others when you enjoy your work or what you do.

advancing your financial development

"Think Rich, Grow Rich" is more than just a catchphrase; it's a philosophy that grows when new opportunities are explored. In this episode, we embark on a voyage of curiosity, venturing into unknown waters in search of opportunities that defy our present comprehension. We explore the art of being curious in unlikely places, accepting unusual viewpoints, and having the courage to try new things. We discover that when we broaden our intellectual horizons, the path to financial success is redrawn through the stories of those who dared to explore new territories.

Three Steps to Open Up New Financial Growth Prospects Step 1: Adopt the Exploration Philosophy Adopt the belief that "Think Rich, Grow Rich" is a philosophy that should be followed and not just a catchphrase. It thrives on continuous exploration of new areas. Acknowledge that financial growth requires taking risks and going outside of the comfort zone. Enter the unknown with an open mind and a sense of excitement by using curiosity as your guide.

Step 2: Seek Out Unusual Information

Make it a challenge to search unexpected sources for knowledge. Investigate ideas and topics that don't seem to relate to your present interests. Acknowledge your ability to make connections between seemingly unconnected concepts. Extending your cognitive reach creates a patchwork of insights that might stimulate original thought and new perspectives on the creation of riches.

Step 3: Take a Chance and Dare to Muster the courage to go into uncharted areas. Recognize discomfort as a sign that you're growing and opening up new opportunities. Draw strength from 3's accounts of those who fearlessly stepped into the unknown. Recognize that you may rewrite the map to financial prosperity and open the door to previously unattainable achievement when you have the guts to venture outside of your comfort zone.

The financial environment is a dynamic tapestry created by market trends. In this segment, we elucidate the significance of learning in adapting to the fluctuations in market dynamics. We look at the ability to monitor, assess, and respond to the developments affecting markets and economic sectors. By analyzing the experiences of people who have endured despite changing circumstances, we uncover the understanding that a mind that is committed to lifelong learning can act as a compass to steer financial endeavors toward successful ends.

Three Steps to Success in Finance: Tracking Market Trends First, cultivate an astute mindset

Understand that the financial environment is always changing due to dynamic market trends. Strive to understand the nuances of market fluctuations and maintain an open mind toward change. Recognize that staying current with these developments is necessary to succeed financially.

Step 2: Develop Your Observational Proficiency

Develop your ability to recognize and assess market trends. Regularly obtain information from dependable sources, examine historical data, and stay abreast of current affairs that affect businesses and economies. By improving your observational abilities, you may provide yourself with the knowledge necessary to make informed decisions in a world that is changing rapidly.

Step 3: Tactical Reaction and Fast Adjustment Recognize market trends and take action to address them. Develop the ability to quickly modify your tactics in reaction to changes in the market. Always be prepared to adjust, veer off course, or seize new chances.

Discover from the experiences of people who have persevered through changing times that constant learning serves as a compass to lead you to financial success in the face of changing market conditions.

Developing an Upbeat Attitude

Positivity is a very useful tool while dealing with hardship. It empowers you to face issues head-on with resilience, optimism, and a firm belief in your capacity to succeed. We'll talk about methods and approaches for developing and sustaining an optimistic outlook in this.

The Influence of Hope

We'll look at how having a positive outlook can improve your resilience, emotional health, and general quality of life. The first step in cultivating positivity is realizing its advantages.

Gratitude Practice: Gratitude is the foundation of an optimistic outlook. We'll explore methods for cultivating thankfulness, such as journaling about your blessings and finding the good in the midst of hardship.

Gratitude in Self-Talk

Your inner voice has a significant impact on your mentality. We'll talk about the value of encouraging self-talk and how to use empowering language to displace self-limiting ideas.

Creating a Growth Mentality

The idea behind an IA growth mentality is that setbacks present chances for development. We'll look at methods for cultivating a growth mentality, which is necessary for resilience in the face of difficulty. You can equip yourself to face hardship with an optimistic heart and an unshakeable spirit by developing a positive mindset. This section

Positivity is a very useful tool while dealing with hardship. It empowers you to face issues head-on with resilience, optimism, and a firm belief in your capacity to succeed. We'll talk about methods and approaches for developing and sustaining an optimistic outlook in this.

The Influence of Hope

We'll look at how having a positive outlook can improve your resilience, emotional health, and general quality of life. The first step in cultivating positivity is realizing its advantages.

Gratitude Exercise

The foundation of a happy outlook is gratitude. We'll explore methods for cultivating thankfulness, such as journaling about your blessings and finding the good in the midst of hardship.

Gratitude in Self-Talk

Your inner voice has a significant impact on your mentality. We'll talk about the value of encouraging self-talk and how to use empowering language to displace self-limiting ideas.

Creating a Growth Mentality

The idea behind an IA growth mentality is that setbacks present chances for development. We'll look at methods for cultivating a growth mentality, which is necessary for resilience in the face of difficulty. You can equip yourself to face hardship with an optimistic heart and an unshakeable spirit by developing a positive mindset. Story 1 in this: Michael Jordan: From Basketball Legend to High School Dropout

Few tales in the annals of sports history are as well-known as Michael Jordan's. His story, which began with him getting cut from his high school basketball team and ended with him becoming an NBA star, is a monument to the human spirit of tenacity.

Put Your Health First

Our general health depends on eating a balanced diet, exercising frequently, and getting adequate sleep. By doing this, further obstacles to a healthy sense of self-worth are also eliminated.

In addition to giving our bodies the nutrition they require to function correctly, eating a balanced diet can lower our chance of developing mental health problems [14]. In fact, the relationship between food and nutrition is the focus of a whole field of psychology. For example, your gastrointestinal tract produces 95% of the serotonin required for mood and sleep regulation. Diets high in sugar have also been connected to the exacerbation of mood disorders, such as depression [15].

In addition to boosting mood and self-esteem, exercise can help lower tension and anxiety.

Getting enough sleep may keep us awake and energized while also replenishing our bodies and minds. More significantly, research has shown that our optimism and sense of self-worth are influenced by the quantity and caliber of our sleep [17]. When I'm tired and sleep-deprived, especially in the evenings when I lie awake at 2 am thinking about my problems, my inner critic is at its worst. Furthermore, it influences our logical decisions and thinking when we are overcome with fatigue.

Taking part in fun and meaningful activities on a regular basis can support our ability to maintain relationships with others and ourselves.

Maintaining your physical health is essential to maintaining your mental and self-worth. Ensure that you give it top consideration. You can start small by introducing a nightly bedtime routine, switching from soda to herbal tea, starting a daily ten-minute walk, or switching from refined white bread to whole wheat.

Acquire the Ability to Apply FAST Theory to Your Decisions

It takes awareness of our activities and deliberate decision-making to make healthy choices. As you learn to make these deliberate decisions to raise your self-esteem, the FAST theory serves as a helpful guide.

➤ F: Treat yourself and other people fairly. You are just as significant as everyone else involved. Strive to keep your assertions factual rather than presumptuous.

➤ A- Don't feel bad about expressing your opinions, disagreeing with others, or having to set boundaries.

➤ S- ADHERE to your principles. Don't give in to pressure from others or compromise with them.

➤ T-Honestly Be True to Both Yourself and Others. Don't embellish or offer justifications. Stay away from small white lies, and don't run from the problem.

Consider the Bond You Have With Your Family.

One's self-esteem can be greatly impacted by family relationships. It serves as the cornerstone of our growth. It can provide us with a solid, self-assured base upon which to stand, or it can make us feel uneasy and nervous. Having a close relationship with our family members can make us feel safe, loved, and like we belong. As a result of feeling more at ease in our surroundings and ourselves, we may experience an increase in self-esteem.

Conversely, a poor relationship with family members might make you feel alone and detached, which lowers your self-worth. Children, in particular, may suffer from this since they may not be able to form a positive sense of who they are and may be more likely to feel inadequate or inferior.

So, how can we raise our self-esteem and family relationships? Cultivating acceptance and understanding is the first step. Ensure that everyone in the family knows they are loved and accepted regardless of what happens. This can foster an atmosphere of safety and security where everyone is treated with respect and value.

Providing chances for family members to interact and connect is also crucial. This could be anything from having dinner together to playing a board game. Family members will have the opportunity to develop stronger bonds and show one another loyalty and trust as a result.

Of course, some of us are in family situations that require more nurturing than a meaningful talk or a family game night. The influence of toxic families or relatives with personality problems on our self-esteem might be significant. Before it's too late, we might not even realize that our self-esteem is suffering. Understanding what is happening and how to address it is crucial.

Making sure you are surrounded by positive people who enhance your best qualities is one method to boost your self-esteem. Make an effort to find and spend time with supportive and upbeat individuals. This can assist in countering any unfavorable signals that your family could be sending your way.

Realizing that you cannot change other people is also crucial. Only you have the power to alter your own conduct. This implies that you must ensure that you are not acting in a way that could undermine your sense of self-worth. This can entail steering clear of particular discussions, staying away from family gatherings, or engaging in activities that make you feel self-conscious. A person may even feel that little to no communication is necessary for their own personal well-being in certain circumstances.

Family Meeting is Tool #4.

Having frequent family meetings is essential to fostering long-lasting relationships with kids and raising their self-esteem and confidence. It will offer the ideal setting for giving and receiving encouragement as well as talking about obstacles and solutions.

It gives kids a great chance to listen to their views and appreciate their feelings, and it gives all family members a sense of duty and belonging. It is incredibly potent because it contributes to a greater sense of cohesion and confidence in the solidity of familial bonds.

Ways to convene a family gathering:

1. Try to have a family gathering once a week.

2. Appoint two relatives to the positions of secretary and chairman.

3. Conduct a meeting with gratitude and praise. Everyone ought to take it one at a time.

The sequence of appreciation and felicitations to the entire family This is a fantastic chance to thank your kids for their efforts and advancements from last week using your new technology.

Additionally, it significantly boosts self-esteem and the sense of being acknowledged.

4. Request that every family share their proudest moments from the most recent gathering. One more massive boost to self-confidence!

5. Take a look at the "agenda," which includes one or more of these items:

Families with individual problems have the chance to voice their needs and identify potential issues.

- Hold a problem-solving workshop to address personal issues.

- Establish the task core system by allocating domestic chores and tasks.

- Organizing family finances and activities.

- Sing a song or play a game. It may sound a little naughty, but giving each other a family embrace at the conclusion of the meeting will strengthen the relationship!

Additional Exercises to Promote Self-Esteem and Self-Confidence:

1. Establish goals and self-awareness

Self-awareness is a fundamental component of self-esteem, as discussed in s 2 and 3, since it helps kids recognize their strengths and develop appropriate expectations for their own abilities. Establishing objectives helps you accomplish your goals over time since it builds self-worth and teaches kids crucial lessons from mistakes.

These are some suggestions to aid in their self-awareness development.

● Request that your youngster list their greatest accomplishments and strengths during a family gathering. Do they think the same things you think about them?

● Request that they discuss one or two objectives or aspirations that they hope to realize in the upcoming year. Ask them to elaborate on the nature of this objective and the process by which it is accomplished. What are the procedures to follow, for instance, if they wish to join the school soccer team or perform in front of an audience within a year? Seek to demonstrate why this is a "fixed way of thinking" and how growth can assist you in reaching your objective if you are making a negative self-assertion.

2. Train the Brain to Function:

It truly aids in the mental development of children since, as discussed in 3, it demonstrates that brain development is possible. It's a terrific approach to demonstrate how synapses form stronger and easier "nervous connections" when they practice new skills.

On YouTube, there are some helpful videos that explain what a development mindset is. Although we disagree with

Class Dojo's app philosophy, these five short video series are extremely well done! Students Growth Mindset - Episode 1/5 - YouTube

3. Enhanced Recollection

Positive memories can increase confidence, as Dominic O'Brien mentioned. From an early age, playing memory games with kids might help them develop better memory.

These games can help you sharpen your memory.

● You are aware of the game. You mentioned that you purchased it in the market. This is an excellent method for improving your memory because it has been shown that telling a tale about a scenario helps individuals remember it. A few begin by saying, "I went to the market and bought it," and then proceed to select the item. Every participant should add new items to the list and read aloud what the other participants said in the appropriate sequence.

● Placing ten objects on the table and asking your youngster to memorize them for one to two minutes is another entertaining and practical activity. After that, turn around and request that they take the thing out. This shortens the amount of time (based on your age) that you can view the objects that are still there and decide which ones you wish to eliminate.

4. Show Them How to Increase Their Confidence by Using Their Bodies

Their confidence may be shown through body language. Teaching kids how to project confidence through body language will have a psychological impact and eventually turn into a self-reinforcing loop.

It is an effective method for lowering tension and anxiety as well as boosting self-assurance when breathing becomes difficult. One of the best methods to lower stress and make logical decisions is to practice deep breathing, often known as belly breathing. Breathing exercises with your children are crucial because they help you control your emotions and reactions to situations. You should practice breathing for three minutes a day, or more, as you become older.

See the Guide to Children Without Manual - Essential Guide to Happy Family Life and Working Parents Guide for further details on the aforementioned resources and methods that can assist radically enhance family life and interactions with children.

Raising a content and self-assured child.

Maintaining And Developing Self-Esteem

Maintaining and growing your sense of self-worth is a lifelong process that needs constant work and attention. We will compile all of the information and techniques covered in this book into one last, giving you a thorough manual for preserving and enhancing your sense of self-worth.

First, Practice Self-Compassion

Establish a self-compassion practice that includes forgiving, understanding, and being kind to yourself. When facing challenges or self-doubt, remember to be kind and patient with yourself. Accept self-compassion as a means of enhancing your sense of worth.

Step 2: Be in the company of uplifting people

By surrounding yourself with good and encouraging individuals, you may create a supportive and pleasant environment for yourself. Spend time with people that are proud of and respect you for who you are. Reduce the amount of time you spend with harmful or poisonous people who can make you feel less confident.

Step 3: Show Appreciation

Develop a grateful mindset by consistently recognizing and appreciating the good things in your life.

Pay more attention to what you have than what you need. Having gratitude improves your perspective and makes you feel more valuable.

Step 4: Take Care of Yourself

Make self-care a priority in order to maintain your mental, emotional, and physical health. Take part in activities that help you feel refreshed and renewed. Allocate time for rest, introspection, and pursuits that make you happy and fulfilled. Your self-esteem grows when you look after yourself.

Step 5: Talk Back to Your Negative Self-Talk

Recognize when you are talking negatively to yourself and use evidence-based reasoning and positive affirmations to counter it. Kindness and self-encouragement should take the place of self-critical ideas. Develop a positive, empowering inner conversation for yourself.

Step 6: Have Reasonable Aspirations

Make sure your goals are reasonable and attainable for yourself. Refrain from striving for perfection and acknowledge that making errors and facing obstacles are inevitable during the process of learning and development. Establish objectives that will challenge you yet are doable for you to feel confident and accomplished.

Step 7: Develop Your Assertiveness

Gaining the ability to articulate your needs, wants, and boundaries clearly requires assertiveness. You may be confident and polite in your expression of yourself without sacrificing your morals or letting people cross your boundaries. Being assertive builds positive relationships and boosts your self-esteem.

Step 8: Honor Your Accomplishments

Celebrate and recognize your accomplishments on a regular basis, no matter how small. Give yourself credit for your efforts and accomplishments, and take some time to acknowledge your improvement. Marking accomplishments gives you confidence and spurs you to keep improving.

Step 9: Welcome introspection

Take regular time to reflect on yourself in order to evaluate your feelings, ideas, and actions. Examine trends and potential areas for development. Accept self-awareness as a tool for self-improvement and self-learning. Take what you've learned from the past and modify it to better fit your objectives and ideals.

Step 10: Engage in Mindfulness Exercises

Make mindfulness a part of your everyday existence. Be in the present moment, devoid of attachment or bias. Be mindful of your thoughts and feelings, studying them with love and curiosity. Being mindful helps you become more aware of and accepting of yourself, which boosts your self-worth.

Step 11: Adopt a Growth Mentality

Embrace a growth attitude that sees your ability to advance personally. Accept difficulties, see failures as teaching moments, and have faith in your capacity to get better with time and effort. Your resilience and sense of self-worth are enhanced by a growth mentality.

Self-esteem building is an ongoing process that calls for perseverance, commitment, and introspection. Through implementing the ideas, methods, and activities presented in this book, you will become more aware of who you are, cultivate steadfast self-worth, and realize your greatest potential. Never forget that you deserve success, respect, and affection. Accept this path, and you'll see an increase in your self-worth.

Present Productive and Healthful Lifestyle Practices

Even while it's obviously important to separate yourself from other people's perceptions of you, other people might occasionally assist you in identifying the aspects of your life that want improvement. You will need to make a significant investment of time to take care of yourself. Since most teenagers live with their parents, it could be reasonable to assume that your caretakers are entirely in charge of your well-being. But as soon as you reach adolescence, that's when you really need to start learning how to take care of yourself and create the life you desire. It is not intended for your caregivers to be in charge of every aspect of your life. It will be up to you to make the necessary investments to create the life you desire. Let's say your goal is to be toned, fit, and have healthy skin. It is up to you, not your caretakers, to work toward this objective. To reach your objective, you must be proactive and take the necessary actions. It's your aim, after all. Your caregivers should provide you with their full support. You will become so content with your life that other people's opinions of you won't really matter when you take the time to build a rich life full of so much progress in your life's social, scholastic, spiritual, emotional, and physical components. However, remarks made by others will have a significant impact on you if your life is full of regrets and misery.

The following suggested lifestyle adjustments, when implemented step-by-step, will enable you to set out on an exciting lifetime journey:

Pay attention to and utilize your strengths: Your mind is constantly working to keep you safe and out of harm's way. This may or may not be beneficial. It's beneficial when it helps you better prepare and prevent mistakes, but it's not beneficial if your fear of failing prevents you from attempting new things. That's why it may be so easy for your mind to go on autopilot and to be inundated with negative thoughts all the time. This is the time when you frequently see the worst in people and situations, which keeps you from moving forward. Develop the ability to control your thoughts, and whenever unfavorable ideas surface, force yourself to resist the need to accept or justify them. Saying aloud, time and time again, the opposite of every negative thought that will be whispering to you is a simple approach to do this. Say aloud something like this whenever you hear your thoughts telling you that trying anything new will make you fail and look foolish: "If I try new things, I am going to excel and have a positive impact in my sphere of influence." You stop surrendering your life and power to a destructive mental program when you take control of your mind in this way.

Imagine yourself leading the life you've always desired. Individuals do actions based on their premeditated thoughts.

Your mind will create a self-fulfilling prophesy if it is always picturing the worst-case scenario. You will begin to see endless chances around you to bring your dreams to reality the more you see yourself living the life you want and experiencing wonderful experiences. Your resources and energy are most likely to go toward what you focus on and talk about frequently. Resilience and self-discipline to regulate your thoughts will help you get this strong attitude more quickly.

Make personal improvement a priority: You can develop into a more competent and better person every day of life. Love discovering new things to learn and being exposed to opportunities for personal development. To have an exciting, rewarding, and fascinating life, one must constantly grow.

Never skip out on getting adequate sleep: Getting enough sleep each day promotes the best possible functioning of the body and mind. It will enable you to give your full attention to the tasks at hand. You'll feel less stressed and be less prone to run into problems when things go well. Sleep deprivation leads to tension and strained eyes. It is a sheer delight to sleep. Make an effort to determine the time you will typically go to bed and wake up. Your mind will wake you up once your body adjusts to this designated hour, so you won't need an alarm to wake you up.

Refrain from spending time and energy on toxic or dangerous people: Your attention is always being reinforced by what you focus on. Refraining from responding to unpleasant people's comments will help you feel more in control of your life. Negative people, like bullies, will probably develop the practice of continuously provoking you once they see how easy it is to alter your mood. They know that by doing this, they will always receive the response they want from you. Bullies should only be addressed if you set clear limits and assert yourself.

Practice self-compassion, grace, and patience: Build the life of your dreams gradually. It takes time to do something worthwhile. Steer clear of self-criticism, and don't undervalue the positive contributions you make to the world every day. Others will learn to be more empathetic toward you the more compassion you demonstrate for yourself.

Make a healthier eating choice and have the guts to refuse unhealthy foods and beverages: Your performance and productivity are greatly impacted by your health. Individuals consume a wide variety of foods and drinks carelessly, often without considering the potential risks to their health. Nowadays, a plethora of information regarding food types may be found online. Examine your present diet in detail. Examine inexpensive dietary adjustments you can make. Handle your body with the same care that a new mother would. Only if the mother is cautious about the food she feeds her infant can the newborn survive. In the same vein, you own your body. It puts forth a lot of effort, day and night, to support you. One surefire method to love and respect oneself is to choose a healthy diet and say no to harmful foods.

This emphasizes the value of regaining control over your life and developing a positive outlook. It can be a complete waste of time and a very harmful habit to care about what other people think of us. You must acknowledge that absent your permission, the majority of the people you may worry about are powerless to steer your path. All of this is your life, and it is a gift. Never let other people's false impressions of you cloud your dreams or make your days less bright. Your self-perception is ultimately what matters, so put your energy and attention into strengthening your bond with yourself. Now that we've covered how to seek the support of people in-depth let's take a brief look at some additional ways you may utilize the support systems in your life and show up courageously every day.

Examining Social Situations: Effective Communication For Self-Observers

Greetings and welcome to "How to Become an Empowered Introvert," Part 2. This section will look at the art of examining social situations and developing strong interpersonal skills that complement your contemplative tendencies. We understand that social media can occasionally feel overwhelming, but with the appropriate strategies and mindset, you can thrive in any group setting while staying true to your authentic self.

Accepting Your Unique Approach to Correspondence

You have a remarkable correspondence style that is perceptive, wise, and compassionate while being a solitary. Accept this communication style and realize its great value in personal and professional interactions. Even if your voice might not be the loudest in the room, your ability to actively listen and offer perceptive thoughts makes you a vital asset in any discussion.

The Power of Complete Focus

Unwavering focus is one of the core skills of considerate individuals in social situations. You can demonstrate genuine interest and create a sense of affiliation by focusing on the speaker. Maintain contact, show understanding with gestures, and provide vocal cues to demonstrate that you are locked in to demonstrate complete attention. This skill helps you build relationships and allows you to gather important information and viewpoints from others.

Astute Responses and Compassionate Writing

Self observers are able to respond with intelligence and empathy. Get some leeway to handle data before disclosing your considerations; this will ensure that your obligations are carefully considered and taken seriously. People may connect with you on a deeper level because of your ability to relate to them, which makes them feel valued and understood. By using these communication skills, you can create real, lifelong relationships with people around you.

Setting Boundaries and Managing Social Energy

Put halting points down to protect your energy because social situations can be draining for considerate people. It's acceptable to turn down requests from time to time and take breaks when needed to recharge. When in doubt, aim higher in your social partnerships, concentrating on meaningful connections that align with your traits and passions. You can better understand and gain respect from your close friends and family if you communicate your wants to them in an open and honest manner.

Overcoming Social Tension

Self-observers may occasionally experience social tension, which might impair their ability to openly connect in friendly situations. Recognize that experiencing anxiety is common and try not to be too hard on yourself. Start with more low-key social events or one-on-one cooperation to gradually ease yourself into friendly exercises as part of openness treatment. Focus on specific outcomes and acknowledge each advancement made.

Using Internet systems administration and innovation

Contemplative individuals can still profit from innovation in their later years. Virtual networks, web-based systems administration courses, and online entertainment provide opportunities to connect and exchange knowledge without the pressure of face-to-face interactions. Accept these opportunities to build relationships and share your ideas and talents.

The Development of Emotional Intelligence

It is common for introverts to naturally lean toward emotional intelligence, which is a necessary ability for successful communication. Being emotionally aware allows you to respond sympathetically and create a positive, stable environment in your social interactions.

Even though introverts cherish their introspective qualities, there are situations that call for assertiveness. Develop decisive correspondence by being open and attentive about your needs, feelings, and boundaries. Remember that being assertive doesn't mean being combative; rather, it means appreciating your voice and making sure it is acknowledged and heard.

As you develop effective communication skills, navigating social situations will become easier and more gratifying for you as an introvert. Remember that your ability to reflect on things can improve your relationships with others and help you form deeper, more meaningful connections.

www.ingramcontent.com/pod-product-compliance
Lightning Source LLC
Chambersburg PA
CBHW052131110526
44591CB00012B/1683